Reading Comprehension

Table of Contents

Glossary	2
Comparison	3
Comprehension	4
Fact or Opinion?	5
Comprehension	6
Comprehension	7
Comparison	8
Review	9
Context	10
Comprehension	11
Recognizing Details	12
Comprehension	13
Context	14
Comprehension	15
Context	16
Main Idea	17
Comprehension	18
Following Directions	19
Comprehension	20
Fact or Opinion?	21
Comprehension	22
Fact or Opinion?	23
Review	24
Recognizing Details	25
Comprehension	26
Following Directions	27
Comprehension	28
Generalization	29
Comprehension	30
Generalization	31
Review	32

Reading Comprehension

Glossary

Comparison. A way to recognize or show how things are alike or different.

Comprehension. Understanding what is seen, heard or read.

Context. A way to figure out the meaning of a new word by relating it to the other words in the sentence.

Fact. A fact can be proved.

Following Directions. Doing what the directions say to do.

Generalization. A generalization is a statement or principle that applies in many different situations.

Main Idea. Finding the most important points.

Opinion. An opinion, which cannot be proved, tells what someone believes.

Recognizing Details. Being able to pick out and remember the who, what, when, where, why and how of what is read.

Reading Comprehension

Comparing Notes On Field Hockey

Comparison is a way to recognize how things are alike or different.

Directions: Read each paragraph, then answer the questions about making comparisons between field hockey, basketball and softball.

My sister is more interested in sports than I am. Last year she lettered in field hockey, basketball and softball. I got my exercise walking to school.

1. What sports did the writer play?

_____

_____

My sister's favorite sport is field hockey. Because it requires constant running up and down a field, it provides more exercise than basketball and softball. There's also more danger, because every year someone gets her teeth knocked out with a hockey stick. So far at our school, no one has lost any teeth to basketball or softball.

2. Compared to basketball and softball, field hockey provides one benefit and one danger. Name them.

_____

_____

On the other hand, softball players—especially those who play the outfield—can occasionally take some time to daydream. With an ace strikeout pitcher and batters who can't hit far, outfielders' gloves don't get much of a workout.

3. What sports **do not** allow time for daydreaming?

_____

_____

Write a short paragraph telling which sport you like best and why.

_____

_____

_____

_____

Reading Comprehension

Name: _____

Comprehension: Floor Exercises For Gymnasts

Have you ever seen gymnasts perform? Their grace and strength is beautiful to see! Good gymnasts make their activities look easy—they never sweat or strain. In reality, it takes enormous strength, agility and flexibility to perform as a gymnast.

At a gymnastics competition, athletes perform these activities: floor exercises, side horse, rings, long horse, parallel bars and horizontal bar. Among these, floor exercises require the most grace and creativity.

Floor exercises are performed in an area that is 39 feet long by 39 feet wide (12 meters by 12 meters). Each gymnast must stay within these lines. If so much as a toe strays outside the area, the judges deduct points from the gymnast's score.

The performance, called a "routine," usually must last only 50 to 70 seconds. Each gymnast's routine must include certain jumping and tumbling activities, or "stunts." Among these are somersaults, jumps, and backwards and forwards handsprings. Each stunt must appear to flow naturally into the next so that the routine looks like it's "all of a piece" instead of a series of random hops and leaps. Music helps set the pace for each gymnast's routine. Because each gymnast chooses different music, it also helps to make each routine distinctive.

Directions: Answer the questions about gymnastics.

1. Name three skills good gymnasts must possess. 1) _____

2) _____ 3) _____

2. How many activities do gymnasts perform at a competition? _____

3. In what size area are floor exercises performed? _____

4. A gymnastic performance is called a

☐ stunt   ☐ competition   ☐ routine

5. Which is not part of a floor routine?

☐ jumps   ☐ rings   ☐ handsprings

Reading Comprehension

Fact Or Opinion?

A fact can be proved. An opinion, which cannot be proved, tells what someone believes.

Directions: Read the numbered sentences and put an x in the corresponding numbered boxes to tell whether each sentence gives a fact or an opinion.

1. Gymnasts are the most exciting athletes to watch!

2. Because their sport requires all-over body strength, gymnasts must have very strong arms and legs. Their stomach muscles and the muscles in their feet must also be in good condition.

3. To do handstands, gymnasts must support the weight of their upside-down bodies by holding their hands flat and their arms straight. Their legs must be pointed straight up.

4. With a little practice, I think anyone could learn to do a handstand.

5. A somersault is more difficult than a handstand.

6. It requires starting and stopping from a standing position after making a 360-degree turn in the air.

7. I'll bet not many people can do a good somersault!

8. Some of the different kinds of somersaults are backwards somersaults, sideways somersaults and something called a "bent body" somersault.

9. I've never seen a bent body somersault, but I think it must require a lot of bending.

10. I don't think I would be any good at the bent body somersault.

1. ☐ Fact ☐ Opinion
2. ☐ Fact ☐ Opinion
3. ☐ Fact ☐ Opinion
4. ☐ Fact ☐ Opinion
5. ☐ Fact ☐ Opinion
6. ☐ Fact ☐ Opinion
7. ☐ Fact ☐ Opinion
8. ☐ Fact ☐ Opinion
9. ☐ Fact ☐ Opinion
10. ☐ Fact ☐ Opinion

Comprehension: Warming Up To Gymnastics

Because no bats, racquets or balls are used, some people mistakenly believe that gymnastics is not a dangerous sport. Although major injuries don't happen often, broken legs—as well as broken necks and backs—can occur. The reason they don't happen frequently is that gymnasts follow safety rules that help prevent accidents.

One thing gymnasts are careful to do every time they practice their sport is to first warm up their muscles. "Warm-ups" are exercises that gently stretch and loosen the muscles before subjecting them to tension and strain.

Warm-ups help the muscles gradually expand and stretch so they move efficiently during vigorous exercise. Without a warm-up of 15 to 30 minutes, it's possible that unworked muscles will be dangerously pulled or strained. Because a muscle injury can interfere with—or stop—an athlete's performance, experienced gymnasts never skip or rush through their warm-ups.

Another thing gymnasts do to help prevent accidents is to use "spotters" when they practice. Spotters are people—usually other gymnasts—who stand beside gymnasts when they are practicing new movements. If gymnasts twist the wrong way or begin to fall, spotters will grab them to prevent injury. Spotters also often offer helpful advice and instant feedback on gymnasts' performances.

Directions: Answer the questions about gymnastics.

1. Name two things gymnasts can do to prevent accidents.

   1.) _____ 2.) _____

2. What's the purpose of a warm-up?

   _____

3. Name three things spotters can do to help gymnasts.

   1.) _____ 2.) _____ 3.) _____

4. Which is not a good length of time for gymnasts to warm up?
   ☐ 5 minutes ☐ 15 minutes ☐ 30 minutes

5. Which is the least likely injury to happen to a gymnast?
   ☐ broken leg ☐ broken back ☐ broken head

Comprehension: Ring Stunts For Gymnasts

Gymnasts who excel at ring stunts must have very strong arms and shoulders. However, gymnastics coaches warn against weightlifting as a way of preparing for using the rings.

Why? Because ring stunts require a delicate combination of balance, coordination and strength. Muscular strength alone is not enough. Coaches say those who first build their muscles weight lifting tend to rely too much on strength and not enough on balance. As a result, their ring performances are not very graceful.

When doing ring stunts, gymnasts must support their entire weight with their arms. If you think this is easy, try doing 10 chin-ups in a row on monkey bars. After number three—if you get that far—you will become a respectful admirer of ring stunts.

An especially difficult ring stunt is called the "wheel." While hanging from the rings, the gymnast turns his body in a full 360 degree circle—a slow "flip." Another very hard stunt is the "hang swing out." In this stunt, the gymnast gets in a handstand position on the rings, then swings down and out by bending and stretching his hips.

At the end of a ring routine, which includes several stunts, a gymnast often gets off the rings via a "somersault dismount." As he hits the peak of the upward movements of a forward swing, he does a somersault in the air before landing with both feet on the floor. The somersault dismount provides a dramatic conclusion to a gymnast's amazingly graceful show of strength and coordination.

Directions: Answer the questions about ring stunts.

1. Why do coaches warn against weight training for ring stunts?

   _____

2. Which ring stunt requires a gymnast to turn in a 360 degree circle?

   _____

3. Which is not a ring stunt?

   ☐ hang swing out   ☐ wheel   ☐ shoulder swing out

4. In the hang swing out, the gymnast first

   ☐ gets in a handstand position   ☐ gets in a wheel position

Reading Comprehension

Name: _____

Comparing Gymnastics Exercises

Directions: Read each paragraph, then answer the questions about making comparisons between ring stunts and floor exercises.

   1. Ring stunts and floor exercises in gymnastics require different kinds of skills. The most obvious difference between the two is that the feet touch the floor in floor exercises.

What do the feet touch in ring stunts? _____

   2. Both floor exercises and ring stunts require graceful movement and the ability to move smoothly from one stunt to another. Ring stunts require great strength in the arms and shoulders. Floor exercises require the gymnast to be sure-footed.

Do floor exercises require great arm and shoulder strength?

_____

   3. Do ring stunts (prior to dismounting) require the gymnast to be

   sure-footed? _____

   4. Because they tend to have stronger upper bodies, men do better in ring exercises than women. However, many spectators insist that women are more exciting performers of floor exercises.

Compared to men, what do women excell at in gymnastics? _____

   5. Because of their smaller size, Japanese men frequently outperform American men on ring stunts. Perhaps because they tend to have longer legs to swing around, American men find mastering ring stunts more of a challenge. This comparison does not hold true for floor exercises.

What factor seems to have no bearing on excelling at floor exercises?

_____

Copyright © 1994 American Education Publishing Co.

Review

When gymnastics became popular at the beginning of this century, ring stunts requiring great strength were the most admired routines. Half a century later after World War II, ring routines grew to include swinging stunts as well. Today, performance on rings is divided into two categories.

The first category includes stunts that emphasize strength, such as holding the legs out straight while pushing the body up with the arms. In the second category are swinging stunts which display quick and graceful movement. Russians were the first gymnasts to perform a swinging stunt on rings. Their performance of "the wheel"—a full body flip—at the 1952 Olympics met with tremendous applause.

As with floor exercises, side horse, long horse, parallel bars and the horizontal bar; mastery of the rings requires a lot of practice. The final goal of all gymnastics routines is to combine a variety of moves and stunts into a performance that shows strength, flexibility and creativity.

Directions: Answer the questions about gymnastics.

1. Compare ring stunts at the turn of the century to gymnastics after World War II.
   _____

2. Compared to the Russians, what did the other gymnasts at the 1952 Olympics lack?
   _____

3. What stunts are in the second category of ring stunts? _____

4. Name six types of stunts.

   1.) _____ 2.) _____ 3.) _____

   4.) _____ 5.) _____ 6.) _____

Fact or opinion?

   Russians are the best gymnasts in the world.   1. ☐ Fact ☐ Opinion

   The Russians were the first to perform swinging stunts.   2. ☐ Fact ☐ Opinion

Reading Comprehension

Name: _____

Context: The Ant and The Cricket

A silly young cricket who decided to sing—
Through the warm sunny months of summer and spring
Began to complain when he found that at home
His **cupboards** were empty and winter had come.

At last by starvation the cricket made bold
To hop through the wintertime snow and the cold
Away he set off to a **miserly** ant
To see if to keep him alive he would **grant**:
Shelter from rain, a mouthful of grain.
"I wish only to borrow—I'll repay it tomorrow—
If not, I must die of starvation and sorrow!"

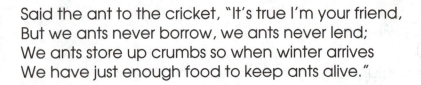

Said the ant to the cricket, "It's true I'm your friend,
But we ants never borrow, we ants never lend;
We ants store up crumbs so when winter arrives
We have just enough food to keep ants alive."

Directions: Answer the questions about the poem.

1. Use context clues to choose the correct definition of "cupboards."

   ☐ where books are stored   ☐ where food is stored   ☐ where shoes are stored

2. Use context clues to choose the correct definition of "miserly."

   ☐ selfish/stingy   ☐ generous/kind   ☐ mean/ugly

3. Use context clues to choose the correct definition of "grant."

   ☐ to take away   ☐ to belch   ☐ to give

Comprehension: Limericks

Old Man From Peru

There was an old man from Peru
Who dreamed he was eating his shoe.
In the midst of the night
He awoke in a fright
And—good grief!—it was perfectly true.

Old Man from Darjeeling

There was an old man from Darjeeling,
Who boarded a bus bound for Ealing.
He saw on the door:
"Please don't spit on the floor."
So he stood up and spat on the ceiling.

Directions: Answer the questions about these silly limericks.

1. In "Old Man From Peru," what was perfectly true?

    _____

2. How did the old man from Peru feel when he awoke?

    _____

3. In "Old Man From Darjeeling," what is Ealing?

    _____

4. What did the old man from Darjeeling see on the door?

    _____

5. Did the old man from Darjeeling break any rules?

    _____

Reading Comprehension Name: _____

Recognizing Details: Tree Toad

A tree toad loved a she-toad
Who lived up in a tree.
He was a two-toed tree toad
But a three-toed toad was she.
The two-toed tree toad tried to win
The three-toed she-toad's heart,
For the two-toed tree toad loved her—
She was lovely, kind and smart.
But the two-toed tree toad loved in vain,
He couldn't coax her down
She stayed alone up in the tree
While he cried on the ground.

Directions: Answer the questions about the poem.

1. How many toes did the female toad have?
_____

2. How many toes did the male toad have?
_____

3. Tell 3 reasons the male toad loved the she-toad.
_____

4. Why was the male toad's love in vain?
_____

5. What did he do in the end?
_____

Comprehension: Three Silly Poems

Poem #1

I eat my peas with honey,
I've done it all my life.
It makes the peas taste funny—
But it keeps them on my knife!

Poem #2

At a restaurant that was quite new
A man found a mouse in his stew
Said the waiter, "Don't shout
Or wave it about,
Or the rest will be wanting one, too!"

Poem #3

If all the world were paper
And all the seas were ink,
And all the trees were bread and cheese,
What would the people think?

Directions: Answer the questions about the silly poems.

1. In poem #1, what's the purpose of the honey?
   _____

2. What's the disadvantage to using honey?
   _____

3. Why did the waiter tell the diner not to shout about the mouse he found?
   _____

4. What were the world, the seas and the trees made of in poem #3?
   _____

Reading Comprehension Name: _____

Context: I Saw A Ship A-Sailing

I saw a ship a-sailing,
A-sailing on the sea.
And, oh! it was all loaded
With tasty things for me.

There was candy in the cabin
And apples in the **hold**;
The sails were made of silk
The **masts** were made of gold.

The four-and-twenty sailors
That stood between the decks,
Were four-and-twenty white mice
With chains around their necks.

The captain was a duck,
With a **packet** on his back.
And when the ship began to move,
The captain said, "Quack! Quack!"

Directions: Answer the questions about the poem.

1. Use context clues to choose the correct definition of "hold."

    ☐ a place inside a ship   ☐ to squeeze or hug   ☐ a tear or rip

2. Use context clues to choose the correct definition of "masts."

    ☐ scarves covering the face   ☐ beams holding up a ship's sails

3. Use context clues to choose the correct definition of "packet."

    ☐ neck chain   ☐ backpack   ☐ two sails

Copyright © 1994 American Education Publishing Co.

Reading Comprehension

Name: _____

Comprehension: Old Gaelic Lullaby

Hush! The waves are rolling in,
White with foam, white with foam,
Father works amid the din.
But baby sleeps at home.

Hush! The winds roar hoarse and deep—
On they come, on they come!
Brother seek the wandering sheep,
But baby sleeps at home.

Hush! The rain sweeps over the fields
Where cattle roam, where cattle roam.
Sister goes to seek the cows
But baby sleeps at home.

Directions: Answer the questions about the Gaelic lullaby. (A Gaelic lullaby is an ancient Irish or Scottish song some parents sing as they rock their babies to sleep.)

1. What is father doing while baby sleeps?
   _____

2. What is brother doing?
   _____

3. What is sister doing?
   _____

4. Is it quiet or noisy while father works?

   ☐ quiet   ☐ noisy

5. Which is **not** mentioned in the poem?

   ☐ wind   ☐ sunshine   ☐ waves   ☐ rain

Reading Comprehension

Name: _____

Context: The Lark And The Wren

"Goodnight, Sir Wren!" said the little lark.
"The daylight fades; it will soon be dark.
I've bathed my wings in the sun's last ray,
I've sung my **hymn** to the parting day.
So now I fly to my quiet glen
In **yonder** meadow—Goodnight Wren!"

"Goodnight, poor Lark," said the **haughty** wren
With a flick of his wing toward his happy friend.
"I also go to my rest **profound**
But not to sleep on the cold, damp ground.
The fittest place for a bird like me
Is the topmost **bough** of a tall pine tree."

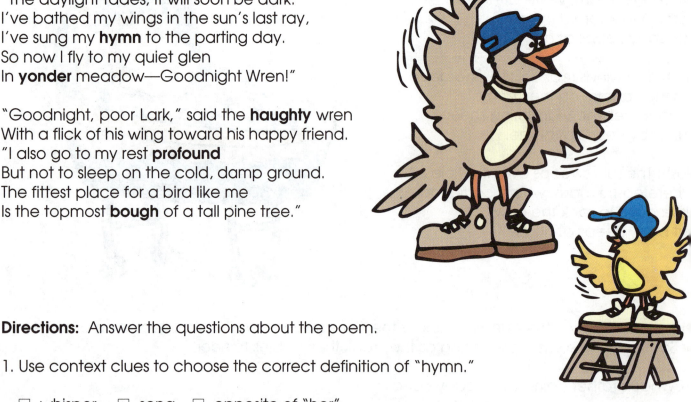

Directions: Answer the questions about the poem.

1. Use context clues to choose the correct definition of "hymn."

   ☐ whisper   ☐ song   ☐ opposite of "her"

2. Use context clues to choose the correct definition of "yonder."

   ☐ nearby   ☐ mountaintop   ☐ seaside

3. Use context clues to choose the correct definition of "haughty."

   ☐ happy   ☐ friendly   ☐ stuck-up

4. Use context clues to choose the correct definition of "profound."

   ☐ restless   ☐ deep   ☐ uncomfortable

5. Use context clues to choose the correct definition of "bough."

   ☐ to bend over   ☐ tree roots   ☐ tree branch

ANSWER KEY

This Answer Key has been designed so that it may be easily removed if you so desire.

GRADE 6 READING COMPREHENSION

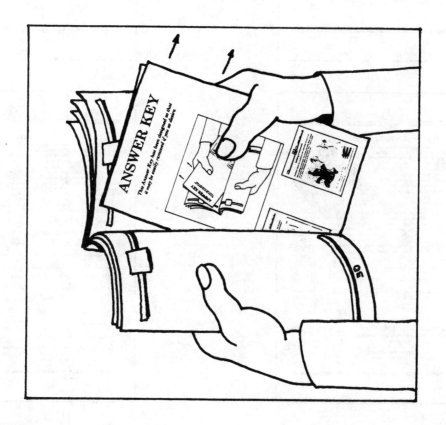

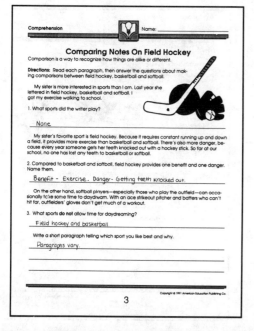

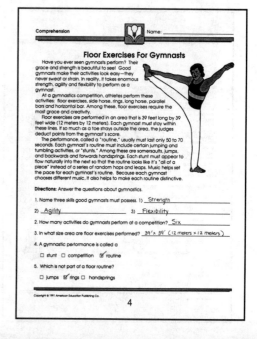

Page 5

Fact Or Opinion?
A fact can be proved. An opinion, which cannot be proved, tells what someone believes.

Directions: Read the numbered sentences and put an x in the corresponding numbered boxes to tell whether each sentence gives a fact or an opinion.

1. Gymnasts are the most exciting athletes to watch! — 1. ☐ Fact ☒ Opinion
2. Because their sport requires all-over body strength, gymnasts must have very strong arms and legs. Their stomach muscles and the muscles in their feet must also be in good condition. — 2. ☒ Fact ☐ Opinion
3. To do handstands, gymnasts must support the weight of their upside-down bodies by holding their hands flat and their arms straight. Their legs must be pointed straight up. — 3. ☒ Fact ☐ Opinion
4. With a little practice, I think anyone could learn to do a handstand. — 4. ☐ Fact ☒ Opinion
5. A somersault is more difficult than a handstand. — 5. ☐ Fact ☒ Opinion
6. It requires starting and stopping from a standing position after making a 360-degree turn in the air. — 6. ☒ Fact ☐ Opinion
7. I'll bet not many people can do a good somersault! — 7. ☐ Fact ☒ Opinion
8. Some of the different kinds of somersaults are backwards somersaults, sideways somersaults and something called a "bent body" somersault. — 8. ☒ Fact ☐ Opinion
9. I've never seen a bent body somersault, but I think it must require a lot of bending. — 9. ☐ Fact ☒ Opinion
10. I don't think I would be any good at the bent body somersault. — 10. ☐ Fact ☒ Opinion

Page 6

Warming Up To Gymnastics

Because no bats, racquets or balls are used, some people mistakenly believe that gymnastics is not a dangerous sport. Although major injuries don't happen often, broken legs—as well as broken necks and backs—can occur. The reason they don't happen frequently is that gymnasts follow safety rules that help prevent accidents.

One thing gymnasts are careful to do every time they practice their sport is to first warm up their muscles. "Warm-ups" are exercises that gently stretch and loosen the muscles before subjecting them to tension and strain.

Warm-ups help the muscles gradually expand and stretch so they move efficiently during vigorous exercise. Without a warm-up of 15 to 30 minutes it's possible that unworked muscles will be dangerously pulled or strained. Because a muscle injury can interfere with—or stop—an athlete's performance, experienced gymnasts never skip or rush through their warm-ups.

Another thing gymnasts do to help prevent accidents is to use "spotters" when they practice. Spotters are people—usually other gymnasts—who stand beside gymnasts when they are practicing new movements. If gymnasts twist the wrong way or begin to fall, spotters will grab them to prevent injury. Spotters also often offer helpful advice and instant feedback on gymnasts' performances.

Directions: Answer the questions about gymnastics.

1. Name two things gymnasts can do to prevent accidents.
   1.) warm up   2.) use spotters
2. What's the purpose of a warm-up?
   Helps muscles gradually expand and stretch.
3. Name three things spotters can do to help gymnasts.
   1.) Grab them to prevent injuries 2.) offer helpful advice 3.) offer instant feedback
4. Which is not a good length of time for gymnasts to warm up?
   ☒ 5 minutes ☐ 15 minutes ☐ 30 minutes
5. Which is the least likely injury to happen to a gymnast?
   ☐ broken leg ☐ broken back ☒ broken head

Page 7

Ring Stunts For Gymnasts

Gymnasts who excel at ring stunts must have very strong arms and shoulders. However, gymnastics coaches warn against weight lifting as a way of preparing for using the rings.

Why? Because ring stunts require a delicate combination of balance, coordination and strength. Muscular strength alone is not enough. Coaches say those who first build their muscles weight lifting tend to rely too much on strength and not enough on balance. As a result, their ring performances are not very graceful.

When doing ring stunts gymnasts must support their entire weight with their arms. If you think this is easy, try doing 10 chin-ups in a row on monkey bars. After number three—if you get that far—you will become a respectful admirer of ring stunts.

An especially difficult ring stunt is called the "wheel." While hanging from the rings, the gymnast turns his body in a full 360 degree circle—a slow "flip." Another very hard stunt is the "hang swing out." In this stunt, the gymnast gets in a handstand position on the rings, then swings down and out by bending and stretching his hips.

At the end of a ring routine, which includes several stunts, a gymnast often gets off the rings via a "somersault dismount." As he hits the peak of the upward movements of a forward swing, he does a somersault in the air before landing with both feet on the floor. The somersault dismount provides a dramatic conclusion to a gymnast's amazingly graceful show of strength and coordination.

Directions: Answer the questions about ring stunts.

1. Why do coaches warn against weight training for ring stunts?
   To prevent too much reliance on strength and not enough on balance.
2. Which ring stunt requires a gymnast to turn in a 360 degree circle?
   Wheel
3. Which is not a ring stunt?
   ☐ hang swing out ☐ wheel ☒ shoulder swing out
4. In the hang swing out, the gymnast first
   ☒ gets in a handstand position ☐ gets in a wheel position

Page 8

Comparing Gymnastics Exercises

Directions: Read each paragraph, then answer the questions about making comparisons between ring stunts and floor exercises.

1. Ring stunts and floor exercises in gymnastics require different kinds of skills. The most obvious difference between the two is that the feet touch the floor in floor exercises.

What do the feet touch in ring stunts? Nothing

2. Both floor exercises and ring stunts require graceful movement and the ability to move smoothly from one stunt to another. Ring stunts require great strength in the arms and shoulders. Floor exercises require the gymnast to be sure-footed.

Do floor exercises require great arm and shoulder strength? No

3. Do ring stunts (prior to dismounting) require the gymnast to be sure-footed? No

4. Because they tend to have stronger upper bodies, men do better in ring exercises than women. However, many spectators insist that women are more exciting performers of floor exercises.

Compared to men, what do women excel at in gymnastics? Floor exercises

5. Because of their smaller size, Japanese men frequently outperform American men on ring stunts. Perhaps because they tend to have longer legs to swing around, American men find mastering ring stunts more of a challenge. This comparison does not hold true for floor exercises.

What factor seems to have no bearing on excelling at floor exercises? Small size

Page 9

Review

When gymnastics became popular at the beginning of this century, ring stunts requiring great strength were the most admired routines. Half a century later after World War II, ring routines grew to include swinging stunts as well. Today, performance on rings is divided into two categories. The first category includes stunts that emphasize strength, such as holding the legs out straight while pushing the body up with the arms. In the second category are swinging stunts which display quick and graceful movement. Russians were the first gymnasts to perform a swinging stunt on rings. Their performance of "the wheel"—a full body flip—at the 1952 Olympics met with tremendous applause.

As with floor exercises, side horse, long horse, parallel bars and the horizontal bar, mastery of the rings requires a lot of practice. The final goal of all gymnastics routines is to combine a variety of moves and stunts into a performance that shows strength, flexibility and creativity.

Directions: Answer the questions about gymnastics.

1. Compare ring stunts at the turn of the century to gymnastics after World War II.
   There were not swinging stunts before WWII.
2. Compared to the Russians, what did the other gymnasts at the 1952 Olympics lack?
   The ability to do swinging stunts.
3. What stunts are in the second category of ring stunts? Swinging stunts
4. Name six types of stunts.
   1.) Ring 2.) floor exercises 3.) side horse
   4.) long horse 5.) parallel bars 6.) horizontal bar

Fact or opinion?
5. Russians are the best gymnasts in the world. 1. ☐ Fact ☒ Opinion
6. The Russians were the first to perform swinging stunts. 2. ☒ Fact ☐ Opinion

Page 10

The Ant And The Cricket

A silly young cricket who decided to sing—
Through the warm sunny months of summer and spring
Began to complain when he found that at home
His **cupboards** were empty and winter had come.

At last by starvation the cricket made bold
To hop through the wintertime snow and the cold
Away he set off to a **miserly** ant
To see if to keep him alive he would **grant**.
Shelter from rain, a mouthful of grain.
"I wish only to borrow—I'll repay if tomorrow;
If not, I must die of starvation and sorrow!"

Said the ant to the cricket, "It's true I'm your friend,
But we ants never borrow, we ants never lend;
We ants store up crumbs so when winter arrives
We have just enough food to keep ants alive."

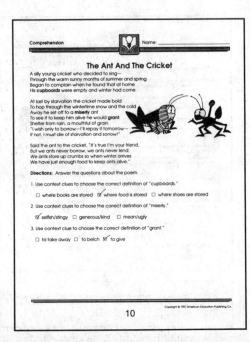

Directions: Answer the questions about the poem.

1. Use context clues to choose the correct definition of "cupboards."
   ☐ where books are stored ☒ where food is stored ☐ where shoes are stored
2. Use context clues to choose the correct definition of "miserly."
   ☒ selfish/stingy ☐ generous/kind ☐ mean/ugly
3. Use context clue to choose the correct definition of "grant."
   ☐ to take away ☐ to belch ☒ to give

Limericks

Old Man From Peru

There was an old man from Peru
Who dreamed he was eating his shoe.
In the midst of the night
He awoke in a fright
And—good grief!—it was perfectly true.

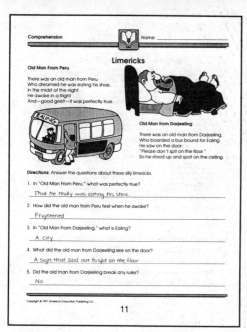

Old Man from Darjeeling

There was an old man from Darjeeling,
Who boarded a bus bound for Ealing.
He saw on the door:
"Please don't spit on the floor."
So he stood up and spat on the ceiling.

Directions: Answer the questions about these silly limericks.

1. In "Old Man From Peru," what was perfectly true?
   That he really was eating his shoe.

2. How did the old man from Peru feel when he awoke?
   Frightened

3. In "Old Man From Darjeeling," what is Ealing?
   A city

4. What did the old man from Darjeeling see on the door?
   A sign that said not to spit on the floor

5. Did the old man from Darjeeling break any rules?
   No

Tree Toad

A tree toad loved a she-toad
Who lived up in a tree.
He was a two-toed tree toad
But a three-toed toad was she.
The two-toed tree toad tried to win
The three-toed she-toad's heart,
For the two-toed tree toad loved her—
She was lovely, kind and smart.
But the two-toed tree toad loved in vain,
He couldn't coax her down
She stayed alone up in the tree
While he cried on the ground.

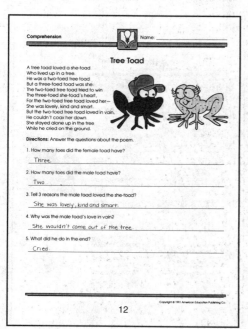

Directions: Answer the questions about the poem.

1. How many toes did the female toad have?
   Three

2. How many toes did the male toad have?
   Two

3. Tell 3 reasons the male toad loved the she-toad.
   She was lovely, kind and smart.

4. Why was the male toad's love in vain?
   She wouldn't come out of the tree.

5. What did he do in the end?
   Cried

Three Silly Poems

Poem #1

I eat my peas with honey,
I've done it all my life.
It makes the peas taste funny—
But it keeps them on my knife!

Poem #2

At a restaurant that was quite new
A man found a mouse in his stew
Said the waiter, "Don't shout
Or wave it about,
Or the rest will be wanting one, too!"

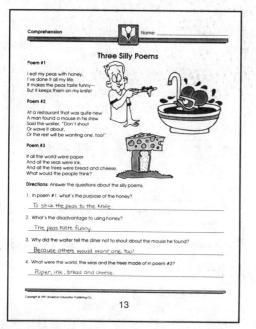

Poem #3

If all the world were paper
And all the seas were ink,
And all the trees were bread and cheese,
What would the people think?

Directions: Answer the questions about the silly poems.

1. In poem #1, what's the purpose of the honey?
   To stick the peas to the knife.

2. What's the disadvantage of using honey?
   The peas taste funny.

3. Why did the waiter tell the diner not to shout about the mouse he found?
   Because others would want one, too!

4. What were the world, the seas and the trees made of in poem #3?
   Paper, ink, bread and cheese.

I Saw A Ship A-Sailing

I saw a ship a-sailing,
A-sailing on the sea.
And, oh! it was all loaded
With tasty things for me.

There was candy in the cabin
And apples in the **hold**;
The sails were made of silk
The **masts** were made of gold.

The four-and-twenty sailors
That stood between the decks,
Were four-and-twenty white mice
With chains around their necks.

The captain was a duck,
With a **packet** on his back.
And when the ship began to move,
The captain said, "Quack! Quack!"

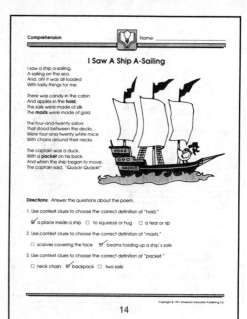

Directions: Answer the questions about the poem.

1. Use context clues to choose the correct definition of "hold."
   ☑ a place inside a ship ☐ to squeeze or hug ☐ a tear or rip

2. Use context clues to choose the correct definition of "masts."
   ☐ scarves covering the face ☑ beams holding up a ship's sails

3. Use context clues to choose the correct definition of "packet."
   ☐ neck chain ☑ backpack ☐ two sails

Old Gaelic Lullaby

Hush! The waves are rolling in,
White with foam, white with foam,
Father works amid the din,
But baby sleeps at home.

Hush! The winds roar hoarse and deep—
On they come, on they come!
Brother seek the wandering sheep,
But baby sleeps at home.

Hush! The rain sweeps over the fields
Where cattle roam, where cattle roam.
Sister goes to seek the cows
But baby sleeps at home.

Directions: Answer the questions about the Gaelic lullaby. (A Gaelic lullaby is an ancient Irish or Scottish song some parents sing as they rock their babies to sleep.)

1. What is father doing while baby sleeps?
   Working

2. What is brother doing?
   Looking for lost sheep.

3. What is sister doing?
   Looking for the cows.

4. Is it quiet or noisy while father works?
   ☐ quiet ☑ noisy

5. Which is **not** mentioned in the poem?
   ☐ wind ☑ sunshine ☐ waves ☐ rain

The Lark And The Wren

"Goodnight, Sir Wren!" said the little lark.
"The daylight fades; it will soon be dark.
I've bathed my wings in the sun's last ray,
I've sung my **hymn** to the parting day.
So now I fly to my quiet glen
In **yonder** meadow—Goodnight Wren!"

"Goodnight poor Lark," said the **haughty** wren
With a flick of his wing toward his happy friend.
"I also go to my rest **profound**
But not to sleep on the cold, damp ground.
The fittest place for a bird like me
Is the topmost **bough** of a tall pine tree."

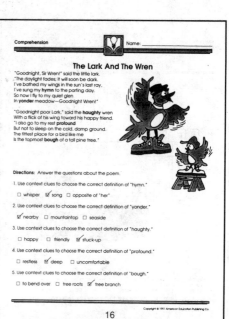

Directions: Answer the questions about the poem.

1. Use context clues to choose the correct definition of "hymn."
   ☐ whisper ☑ song ☐ opposite of "her"

2. Use context clues to choose the correct definition of "yonder."
   ☑ nearby ☐ mountaintop ☐ seaside

3. Use context clues to choose the correct definition of "haughty."
   ☐ happy ☐ friendly ☑ stuck-up

4. Use context clues to choose the correct definition of "profound."
   ☐ restless ☑ deep ☐ uncomfortable

5. Use context clues to choose the correct definition of "bough."
   ☐ to bend over ☐ tree roots ☑ tree branch

The Gettysburg Address

On November 19, 1863, President Abraham Lincoln gave a short speech to dedicate a cemetery of Civil War soldiers in Gettysburg, Pennsylvania where a famous battle was fought. He wrote five drafts of the Gettysburg Address, one of the most stirring speeches of all time. The war ended in 1865.

Four score and seven years ago our fathers brought forth on this continent, a new nation, conceived in liberty, and dedicated to the proposition that all men are created equal.

Now we are engaged in a great civil war, testing whether that nation, or any nation so conceived and so dedicated, can long endure. We are met on a great battlefield of that war. We have come to dedicate a portion of that field as a final resting place for those who here gave their lives that this nation might live. It is altogether fitting and proper that we should do this.

But, in a larger sense, we cannot dedicate - we cannot consecrate - we cannot hallow - this ground. The brave men, living and dead, who struggled here have consecrated it far above our poor power to add or detract. The world will little note nor long remember what we say here, but it can never forget what they did here. It is for us the living, rather, to be dedicated to the unfinished work which they who fought here have thus far so nobly advanced. It is rather for us to be here dedicated to the great task remaining before us - that from these honored dead we take increased devotion to that cause for which they gave the last full measure of devotion - that we here highly resolve that these dead shall not have died in vain - that this nation, under God, shall have a new birth of freedom - and that government of the people, by the people, for the people shall not perish from this earth.

Directions: Answer the questions about the Gettysburg Address.

1. The main idea is
   - ☐ This speech will be long remembered as a tribute to the dead who died fighting in the Civil War.
   - ✓ This speech is to honor the dead soldiers who gave their lives so that the nation could have freedom for all citizens.

2. What battle was fought on the ground where the cemetery stood?
   Gettysburg

The Emancipation Proclamation

On September 22, 1862—a year before delivering the Gettysburg Address President Lincoln delivered The Emancipation Proclamation, which stated that all slaves in Confederate states should be set free. Since the Confederate states had already withdrawn from the Union, they of course ignored the Proclamation. The Proclamation did strengthen the north's war effort. About 200,000 black men—mostly former slaves—enlisted in the Union Army. Two years later the 13th Amendment to the Constitution ended slavery in all parts of the United States.

I, Abraham Lincoln, do order and declare that all persons held as slaves within said designated States and parts of States are, and henceforward shall be, free; and that the Executive Government of the United States, including military and naval authorities thereof, shall recognize and maintain the freedom of said persons.

And I hereby enjoin upon the people so declared to be free to abstain from all violence, unless in necessary self-defense; and I recommend to them that, in all cases where allowed, they labor faithfully for reasonable wages.

And I further declare and make known that such persons of suitable condition will be received into the armed forces of the United States to garrison forts, positions, stations, and other places, and to man vessels of all sorts in said service.

(This is not the full text of the Emancipation Proclamation.)

Directions: Answer the questions about the Emancipation Proclamation.

1. How did the Emancipation Proclamation strengthen the north's war effort?
   By allowing black men to join the Union Army - 200,000 of them did

2. Which came first, the Emancipation Proclamation or the Gettysburg Address?
   Emancipation Proclamation

3. Which amendment to the constitution grew out of the Emancipation Proclamation?
   13th Amendment

Puzzling Out The Proclamation

Directions: Use the facts you learned about the Emancipation Proclamation to work the puzzle.

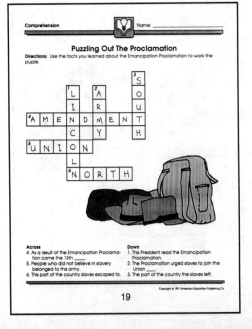

Across
1. As a result of the Emancipation Proclamation came the 13th ____.
5. People who did not believe in slavery belonged to this army.
6. This part of the country slaves escaped to.

Down
1. This President read the Emancipation Proclamation.
2. The Proclamation urged slaves to join the Union ____.
3. The part of the country the slaves left.

Lincoln And The Southern States

Many people think that Abraham Lincoln had publicly come out against slavery from the beginning of his term as president. This is not the case. Whatever his private feelings, publicly he did not criticize slavery. Fearful that the southern states would secede, or leave, the union, he pledged to respect the southern states' rights to own slaves. He also pledged that the government would respect the southern states' runaway slave laws. These laws required all citizens to return runaway slaves to their masters.

Clearly, Lincoln did not want the country torn apart by a civil war. In the following statement, written in 1861 shortly after he became president, he makes it clear that the federal government will do its best to avoid conflict with the southern states.

I hold that, in contemplation of the universal law and of the Constitution, the Union of these states is perpetual. . . No state, upon its own mere motion, can lawfully get out of the Union. . . . I shall take care, as the Constitution itself expressly enjoins upon me, that the laws of the Union be faithfully executed in all the states. . . . The power confided to me will be used to hold, occupy, and possess the property and places belonging to the government, and to collect the duties and imposts. . . .

In your hands, my dissatisfied fellow-countrymen, and not in mine, is the momentous issue of civil war. The government will not assail you. You can have no conflict without yourselves being the aggressors. You have no oath registered in heaven to destroy the government, while I shall have the most solemn one to "preserve protect and defend" it.

Directions: Answer the questions about Lincoln and the southern states.

1. Use a dictionary to find the definition of "assail." _Physically attack_

2. Use a dictionary to find the definition of "enjoin." _To order_

3. Use a dictionary to find the definition of "contemplation." _The study of_

4. Lincoln is telling the southern states that the government
   - ☐ does want a war ✓ doesn't want a war ☐ will stop a war

5. As president, Lincoln pledged to "preserve, protect and defend"
   - ☐ slavery ☐ the northern states ✓ the union

Fact Or Opinion?

Directions: Read the numbered sentences and put an x in the corresponding numbered boxes to tell whether each sentence gives a fact or an opinion.

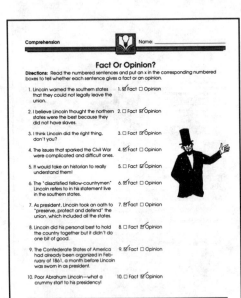

1. Lincoln warned the southern states that they could not legally leave the union. 1. ✓ Fact ☐ Opinion

2. I believe Lincoln thought the northern states were the best because they did not have slaves. 2. ☐ Fact ✓ Opinion

3. I think Lincoln did the right thing, don't you? 3. ☐ Fact ✓ Opinion

4. The issues that sparked the Civil War were complicated and difficult ones. 4. ✓ Fact ☐ Opinion

5. It would take an historian to really understand them! 5. ☐ Fact ✓ Opinion

6. The "dissatisfied fellow-countrymen" Lincoln refers to in his statement live in the southern states. 6. ✓ Fact ☐ Opinion

7. As president, Lincoln took an oath to "preserve, protect and defend" the union, which included all the states. 7. ✓ Fact ☐ Opinion

8. Lincoln did his personal best to hold the country together but it didn't do one bit of good. 8. ☐ Fact ✓ Opinion

9. The Confederate States of America had already been organized in February of 1861, a month before Lincoln was sworn in as president. 9. ✓ Fact ☐ Opinion

10. Poor Abraham Lincoln—what a crummy start to his presidency! 10. ☐ Fact ✓ Opinion

---

Away Down South In Dixie

Although many southerners disapproved of slavery, the pressure to go along with the majority who supported slavery was very strong. Many of those who thought slavery was wrong did not talk about their opinions. It was dangerous to do so!

The main reason the southern states seceded (withdrew) from the union in 1861 was because they wanted to protect their right to own slaves. They also wanted to increase the number of slaves so they could increase production of cotton and other crops that slaves tended. Many Civil War monuments in the south are dedicated to a war that was described as "just and holy."

"Dixie," a song written in 1859 that is still popular in the south, sums up the attitude of many southerners. As the song lyrics show, southerners' loyalties lay not with the union representing all the states, but with the south and the southern way of life.

Dixie
I wish I was in Dixie, Hoo-ray! Hoo-ray!
In Dixie land I'll take my stand
To live and die in Dixie.
Away, away, away down south in Dixie!
Away, away, away down south in Dixie!
(This is not the full text of the song.)

Directions: Answer the questions about Southerners and "Dixie".

1. Why did southerners who disapproved of slavery keep their opinions to themselves?
   It was dangerous to disagree.

2. Why did southerners want more slaves?
   So they could increase production of cotton and other crops.

3. What are the words on some southern Civil War monuments?
   Just and holy.

4. What "stand" is referred to in Dixie?
   ✓ stand for slavery ☐ stand against slavery ☐ stand for cotton

5. "Secede" means to
   ☐ quit ☐ fight ✓ withdraw

Fact Or Opinion?

Directions: Read the numbered sentences and put an x in the corresponding numbered boxes to tell whether each sentence gives a fact or an opinion.

1. Dixie is a beautiful song! — 1. ☐ Fact ☒ Opinion
2. It was written in 1859 by a man named Daniel Emmett, who died in 1904. — 2. ☒ Fact ☐ Opinion
3. The song became a rallying cry for southerners because it showed where their loyalties were. — 3. ☒ Fact ☐ Opinion
4. I think their loyalty to slavery was absolutely wrong! — 4. ☐ Fact ☒ Opinion
5. These four states where people owned slaves did not secede from the Union: Delaware, Maryland, Kentucky and Missouri. — 5. ☒ Fact ☐ Opinion
6. The people in these states certainly made the right moral choice. — 6. ☐ Fact ☒ Opinion
7. The ownership of one human being by another is absolutely and totally wrong under any circumstances. — 7. ☐ Fact ☒ Opinion
8. In the states that did not secede from the union, some people fought for the Union and others fought for the Confederacy of Southern States. — 8. ☒ Fact ☐ Opinion
9. Sometimes brothers fought against brothers on opposite sides of the war. — 9. ☒ Fact ☐ Opinion
10. What a horrible situation to be in! — 10. ☐ Fact ☒ Opinion

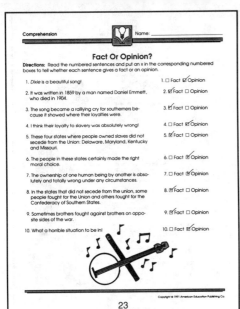

Photography Terms

Like other good professionals, photographers make their craft look easy. Their skill—like that of the graceful ice skater—comes from years of practice. Where skaters develop a sense of balance, photographers develop an "eye" for pictures. They can make important technical decisions about a photograph, or "shooting," a particular scene in the twinkling of an eye.

It's interesting to know some of the technical language that professional photographers use. "Angle of view" refers to the angle from which a photograph is taken. "Depth of field" is the distance between the nearest point and the farthest point in a photo that is in focus.

"Filling the frame" refers to the amount of space the object being photographed takes up in the picture. A close-up picture of a dog, flower or person would fill the frame. A far-away picture would not.

"ASA" refers to the speed of different types of films. "Speed" means the film's sensitivity to light. The letters ASA stand for the American Standards Association. Film manufacturers give their films ratings of 200ASA, 400ASA, etc. to indicate film speed. The higher the number on the film, the higher its sensitivity to light and the faster its speed. The faster its speed, the better it will be at clearly capturing sports images and other action shots.

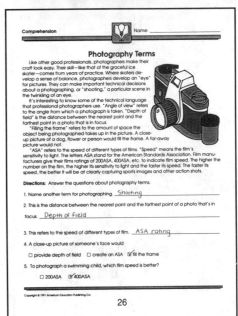

Directions: Answer the questions about photography terms.

1. Name another term for photographing. _Shooting_
2. This is the distance between the nearest point and the farthest point of a photo that's in focus. _Depth of field_
3. This refers to the speed of different types of film. _ASA rating_
4. A close-up picture of someone's face would
   ☐ provide depth of field ☐ create an ASA ☒ fill the frame
5. To photograph a swimming child, which film speed is better?
   ☐ 200ASA ☒ 400ASA

Review

Although they were outnumbered, most southerners were convinced they could win the Civil War. The white population of the southern states was 5.5 million. The population was 18.9 million in the 19 states that stayed with the Union. Despite these odds, southerners felt history was on their side.

After all, the Colonists had been the underdogs against the British and had won the war for independence. Europeans also felt that Lincoln could not force the South to re-join the Union. The United Netherlands had successfully seceded from Spain. Greece had seceded from Turkey. Europeans were laying odds that two countries would take the place of what had once been the United States.

Directions: Answer the questions and work the puzzle.

1. What was the difference in population between the Union and Confederate states? _13.4 million_

2. The main idea is
   ✓ Although they were outnumbered, many people here and abroad felt the South would win the Civil War.
   ☐ Because they were outnumbered, the South knew winning the Civil War was a very long shot.

Across
4. They won the war of independence against England.
5. Did Europeans believe the South would win the war?
6. _____ teen states belonged to the Union.

Down
1. Slaveowners lived in this area of the country.
2. The president during the Civil War.
3. To withdraw from the Union.

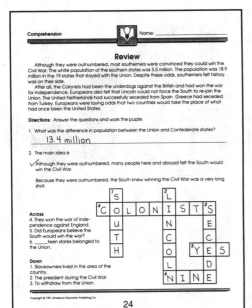

Photography Puzzler

Directions: Use the facts you have learned about photography to work the puzzle.

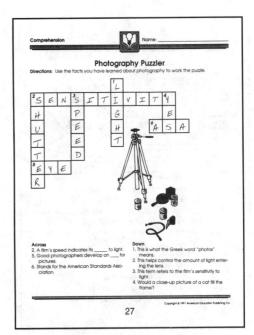

Across
2. A film's speed indicates its _____ to light.
5. Good photographers develop an _____ for pictures.
6. Stands for the American Standards Association.

Down
1. This is what the Greek word "photos" means.
2. This helps control the amount of light entering the lens.
3. This term refers to the film's sensitivity to light.
4. Would a close-up picture of a cat fill the frame?

Fun With Photography

The word photography means "writing with light." "Photo" is from the Greek word **photos** which means light. "Graphy" is from the Greek word **graphic** which means writing. Cameras don't literally write pictures of course. Instead, they imprint an image onto a piece of film.

Even the most sophisticated camera is basically a box with a piece of light sensitive film inside a box. The box has a hole at the opposite end from the film. The light enters the box from the hole—the camera's lens—and shines on the surface of the film to create a picture. The picture that's created on the film is the image the camera's lens is pointed toward.

A **lens** is a circle of glass that is thinner at the edges and thicker in the center. The outer edges of the lens collect the light rays and draw them together at the center of the lens.

The **shutter** helps control the amount of light that enters the lens. Too much light will make the picture too light. Too little light will result in a dark picture. Electronic flash—built into the camera or attached to the top of it—provides light when needed.

Cameras with automatic electronic flashes will provide the additional light automatically. Electronic flashes—or "flashes" as they are often called—require batteries. If your automatic flash or flash attachment quits working, a dead battery is probably the cause.

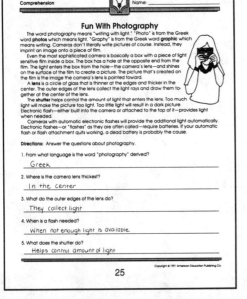

Directions: Answer the questions about photography.

1. From what language is the word "photography" derived? _Greek_
2. Where is the camera lens thickest? _In the center_
3. What do the outer edges of the lens do? _They collect light_
4. When is a flash needed? _When not enough light is available_
5. What does the shutter do? _Helps control amount of light_

Photographing Animals

Animals are a favorite subject of many young photographers. Cats, dogs, hamsters and other pets top the list, followed by zoo animals and the occasional lizard.

Because it's hard to get them to sit still and "perform on command," many professional photographers joke that—given a choice—they will refuse to photograph pets or small children. There **are** ways around the problem of short attention spans, however.

One way to get an appealing portrait of a cat or dog is to hold a biscuit or treat above the camera. The animal's longing look toward the food will be captured by the camera as a soulful gaze.

Because it's above the camera—out of the camera's range—the treat won't appear in the picture. When you show the picture to your friends afterwards they will be impressed by your pet's loving expression.

If you are using fast film, you can take some good, quick shots of pets by simply snapping a picture right after calling their names. You'll get a different expression from your pet using this technique. Depending on your pet's disposition, the picture will capture an inquisitive expression or possibly a look of annoyance—especially if you've awakened Rover from a nap!

To photograph zoo animals, put the camera as close to the animal's cage as possible so you can shoot between the bars or wire mesh. Wild animals don't respond the same way as pets—after all, they don't know you!—so you will have to be more patient to capture a good shot. If it's legal to feed the animals, you can get their attention by having a friend toss them treats as you concentrate on shooting some good pictures.

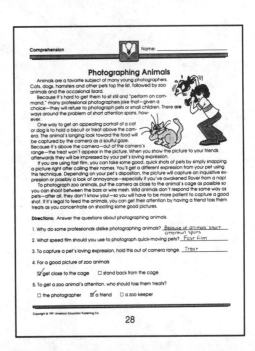

Directions: Answer the questions about photographing animals.

1. Why do some professionals dislike photographing animals? _Because of animals short attention spans_
2. What speed film should you use to photograph quick-moving pets? _Fast film_
3. To capture a pet's loving expression, hold this out of camera range. _Treat_
4. For a good picture of zoo animals,
   ☒ get close to the cage ☐ stand back from the cage
5. To get a zoo animal's attention, who should toss them treats?
   ☐ the photographer ☒ a friend ☐ a zoo keeper

Generalization

A generalization is a statement of principle that applies in many different situations.

Directions: Read each passage and circle the valid generalization.

1. Most people can quickly be taught to use a simple camera. However, it takes time, talent and a good eye to learn to take professional quality photographs. Patience is another quality that good photographers must possess. Those who photograph nature often will wait hours to get just the right light or shadow in their pictures.

   a. There's no one who can't learn to use a camera.
   b. Any patient person can become a good photographer.
   c. (Good photographers have a good eye for pictures.)

2. Photographers such as Diane Arbus, who photograph strange or odd people, also must wait for just the right picture. Many "people photographers" stake out a busy city sidewalk and study the faces of crowds. Then they must leap up quickly and ask to take a picture—or sneakily take one without being observed. Either way, it's not an easy task!

   a. Staking out a busy city sidewalk is a boring task.
   b. ("People photographers" must be patient people and good observers.)
   c. Sneak photography is not a nice thing to do to strangers.

3. Whether the subject is nature or humans, many photographers insist that dawn is the best time to take pictures. The light is clear at this early hour, and mist may still be in the air. The mist gives these early morning photos a haunting, "other world" quality that is very appealing.

   a. (Morning mist gives an unusual quality to most outdoor photographs.)
   b. Photographers all agree that dawn is the best time to take pictures.
   c. Misty light is always important in taking all pictures.

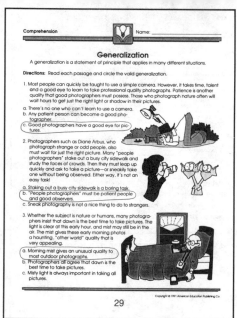

29

Generalization

Directions: Read each passage and circle the valid generalization.

1. Professional photographers know it's important to keep their cameras clean and in good working order. Amateur photographers should make sure theirs are, too. However, to take good care of your camera, you must first understand the equipment. Camera shop owners say at least half the "defective" cameras people bring in simply need to have the battery changed!

   a. Cameras are delicate and require constant care so they will work properly.
   b. (Many problems amateurs have are caused by lack of familiarity with their equipment.)
   c. Amateur photographers don't know how their cameras work.

2. Once a year, some people take their cameras to a shop to be cleaned. Most never have them cleaned at all! Those who know how can clean their cameras themselves. To avoid scratching the lens, they should use the special cloths and tissues professionals rely on. Amateurs are warned never to unloosen screws, bolts or nuts inside the camera.

   a. (The majority of amateur photographers never bother to have their cameras cleaned.)
   b. Cleaning a camera can be tricky and should be left to professionals.
   c. It's hard to find the special cleaning cloths professionals use.

3. Another simple tip from professionals—make sure your camera works **before** you take it on vacation. They suggest taking an entire roll of film and having it developed before your trip. That way, if necessary, you'll have time to have the lens cleaned or other repairs made.

   a. (Check out your camera beforehand to make sure it's in good working order before you travel.)
   b. Vacation pictures are often disappointing because the camera needs repairing.
   c. Take at least one roll of film along on every vacation.

31

Camera Care

Camera dealers say many amateur photographers should take better care of their cameras. Too often, people carelessly leave expensive cameras laying out where young children or pets can get hold of them. They fail to keep put cameras back into the carrying cases that protect them. They take them to the beach and leave them laying in the sand. Another way people ruin their cameras is by leaving them for days inside a hot car.

Because they must carry so many attachments, professional photographers keep their cameras inside a large, soft shoulder bag. The bag provides extra protection for the camera, which is also protected by its camera case.

Inside the bag are compartments for film, extra lenses and other attachments. Other equipment inside a professional photographer's bag may include the following: lens hood, cable release, filters and holder, cleaning cloth and screw driver. A photographer's bag is filled with all sorts of interesting things!

Flashlights, pens, tape and sometimes a sandwich for lunch may fill out the odd assortment of objects. In addition, many photographers carry a tripod to set the camera on for still pictures. Can you see why photographers usually develop strong arm and shoulder muscles?

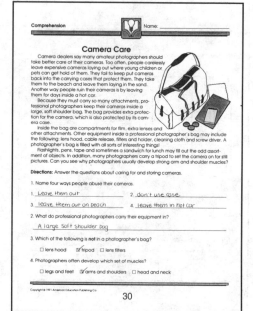

Directions: Answer the questions about caring for and storing cameras.

1. Name four ways people abuse their cameras.
   1. Leave them out
   2. don't use case
   3. leave them out on beach
   4. leave them in hot car

2. What do professional photographers carry their equipment in?
   A large soft shoulder bag

3. Which of the following is **not** in a photographer's bag?
   ☐ lens hood ☒ tripod ☐ lens filters

4. Photographers often develop which set of muscles?
   ☐ legs and feet ☒ arms and shoulders ☐ head and neck

30

Review

Using A Darkroom

The room where photographs are developed is called a "darkroom." Can you guess why? The room must be completely dark so that light does not get on the film as it is being developed. Because of the darkness and the chemicals used in the developing process, it's important to follow certain darkroom safety procedures.

To avoid shocks while in the darkroom, never touch light switches with wet hands. To avoid touching chemicals, use tongs to transfer prints from one chemical solution to another. When finished with the chemicals, put them back in their bottles. Never leave chemicals out in trays once the developing process is completed.

To avoid skin irritation from chemicals, wipe down all counter tops and surfaces when finished. Another sensible precaution—make sure you have everything you need **before** exposing the film to begin the developing process. Any light that enters the darkroom as you leave to get a forgotten item can ruin the pictures being developed.

Directions: Answer the questions about using a darkroom.

1. Which generalization is correct?
   a. Developing pictures is a time-consuming and difficult process.
   b. It's dangerous to develop pictures in a darkroom.
   c. (Sensible safety procedures are important for darkroom work.)

2. Give directions for working with photography chemicals.
   Use tongs, put them back when done, wipe counters

3. Give the most important detail on how to make sure pictures aren't ruined in the darkroom.
   Don't open the door!

32

Main Idea: The Gettysburg Address

On November 19, 1863, President Abraham Lincoln gave a short speech to dedicate a cemetery of Civil War soldiers in Gettysburg, Pennsylvania where a famous battle was fought. He wrote five drafts of the Gettysburg Address, one of the most stirring speeches of all time. The war ended in 1865.

Four score and seven years ago our fathers brought forth on this continent, a new nation, conceived in liberty, and dedicated to the proposition that all men are created equal.

Now we are engaged in a great civil war, testing whether that nation, or any nation so conceived and so dedicated, can long endure. We are met on a great battlefield of that war. We have come to dedicate a portion of that field as a final resting place for those who here gave their lives that this nation might live. It is altogether fitting and proper that we should do this.

But, in a larger sense, we cannot dedicate - we cannot consecrate - we cannot hallow - this ground. The brave men, living and dead, who struggled here have consecrated it far above our poor power to add or detract. The world will little note nor long remember what we say here, but it can never forget what they did here. It is for us the living, rather, to be dedicated to the unfinished work which they who fought here have thus far so nobly advanced. It is rather for us to be here dedicated to the great task remaining before us - that from these honored dead we take increased devotion to that cause for which they gave their last full measure of devotion - that we here highly resolve that these dead shall not have died in vain - that this nation, under God, shall have a new birth of freedom - and that government of the people, by the people, for the people shall not perish from this earth.

Directions: Answer the questions about the Gettysburg Address.

1. The main idea is

   This speech will be long remembered as a tribute to the dead who died fighting in the Civil War.

   This speech is to honor the dead soldiers who gave their lives so that the nation could have freedom for all citizens.

2. What battle was fought on the ground where the cemetery stood?

_____

Comprehension: The Emancipation Proclamation

On September 22, 1862—a year before delivering the Gettysburg Address—President Lincoln delivered the Emancipation Proclamation, which stated that all slaves in Confederate states should be set free. Since the Confederate states had already withdrawn from the Union, they of course ignored the Proclamation. The proclamation did strengthen the north's war effort. About 200,000 black men—mostly former slaves—enlisted in the Union Army. Two years later, the 13th Amendment to the Constitution ended slavery in all parts of the United States.

I, Abraham Lincoln, do order and declare that all persons held as slaves within said designated States and parts of States are, and henceforward shall be, free; and that the Executive Government of the United States, including military and naval authorities thereof, shall recognize and maintain the freedom of said persons.

And I hereby enjoin upon the people so declared to be free to abstain from all violence, unless in necessary self-defense; and I recommend to them that, in all cases where allowed, they labor faithfully for reasonable wages.

And I further declare and make known that such persons of suitable condition will be received into the armed forces of the United States to garrison forts, positions, stations, and other places, and to man vessels of all sorts in said service.

(This is not the full text of the Emancipation Proclamation.)

Directions: Answer the questions about the Emancipation Proclamation.

1. How did the Emancipation Proclamation strengthen the north's war effort?

_____

2. Which came first, the Emancipation Proclamation or the Gettysburg Address?

_____

3. Which amendment to the constitution grew out of the Emancipation Proclamation?

_____

Reading Comprehension

Name: _____

Following Directions: Puzzling Out The Proclamation

Directions: Use the facts you learned about the Emancipation Proclamation to work the puzzle.

Across

4. As a result of the Emancipation Proclamation came the 13th _____.
5. People who did not believe in slavery belonged to this army.
6. The part of the country to which slaves escaped.

Down

1. This President read the Emancipation Proclamation.
2. The Proclamation urged slaves to join the Union _____.
3. The part of the country the slaves left.

Reading Comprehension

Name: _____

Comprehension: Lincoln And The Southern States

Many people think that Abraham Lincoln had publicly come out against slavery from the beginning of his term as president. This is not the case. Whatever his private feelings, publicly he did not criticize slavery. Fearful that the southern states would secede, or leave, the union, he pledged to respect the southern states' rights to own slaves. He also pledged that the government would respect the southern states' runaway slave laws. These laws required all citizens to return runaway slaves to their masters.

Clearly, Lincoln did not want the country torn apart by a civil war. In the following statement, written in 1861 shortly after he became president, he made it clear that the federal government would do its best to avoid conflict with the southern states.

I hold that, in contemplation of the universal law and the Constitution, the Union of these states is perpetual. . . No state, upon its own mere motion, can lawfully get out of the Union. . . . I shall take care, as the Constitution itself expressly enjoins upon me, that the laws of the Union be faithfully executed in all the states. . . . The power confided to me will be used to hold, occupy, and possess the property and places belonging to the government, and to collect the duties and imposts. . . .

In your hands, my dissatisfied fellow-countrymen, and not in mine, is the momentous issue of civil war. The government will not assail you. You can have no conflict without yourselves being the aggressors. You have no oath registered in heaven to destroy the government, while I shall have the most solemn one to "preserve protect and defend" it.

Directions: Answer the questions about Lincoln and the southern states.

1. Use a dictionary to find the definition of "assail." _____

2. Use a dictionary to find the definition of "enjoin." _____

3. Use a dictionary to find the definition of "contemplation." _____

4. Lincoln is telling the southern states that the government

   ☐ does want a war   ☐ doesn't want a war   ☐ will stop a war

5. As president, Lincoln pledged to "preserve, protect and defend"

   ☐ slavery   ☐ the northern states   ☐ the union

Reading Comprehension

Name: _____

Fact Or Opinion?

Directions: Read the numbered sentences and put an x in the corresponding numbered boxes to tell whether each sentence gives a fact or an opinion.

1. Lincoln warned the southern states that they could not legally leave the union.

    1. ☐ Fact ☐ Opinion

2. I believe Lincoln thought the northern states were the best because they did not have slaves.

    2. ☐ Fact ☐ Opinion

3. I think Lincoln did the right thing, don't you?

    3. ☐ Fact ☐ Opinion

4. The issues that sparked the Civil War were complicated and difficult ones.

    4. ☐ Fact ☐ Opinion

5. It would take an historian to really understand them!

    5. ☐ Fact ☐ Opinion

6. The "dissatisfied fellow-countrymen" Lincoln refers to in his statement lived in the southern states.

    6. ☐ Fact ☐ Opinion

7. As president, Lincoln took an oath to "preserve, protect and defend" the union, which included all the states.

    7. ☐ Fact ☐ Opinion

8. Lincoln did his personal best to hold the country together, but it didn't do one bit of good.

    8. ☐ Fact ☐ Opinion

9. The Confederate States of America had already been organized in February of 1861, a month before Lincoln was sworn in as president.

    9. ☐ Fact ☐ Opinion

10. Poor Abraham Lincoln—what a crummy start to his presidency!

    10. ☐ Fact ☐ Opinion

Comprehension: Away Down South In Dixie

Although many southerners disapproved of slavery, the pressure to go along with the majority who supported slavery was very strong. Many of those who thought slavery was wrong did not talk about their opinions. It was dangerous to do so!

The main reason the southern states seceded (withdrew) from the union in 1861 was because they wanted to protect their right to own slaves. They also wanted to increase the number of slaves so they could increase production of cotton and other crops that slaves tended. Many Civil War monuments in the south are dedicated to a war that was described as "just and holy."

"Dixie," a song written in 1859 that is still popular in the south, sums up the attitude of many southerners. As the song lyrics show, southerners' loyalties lay not with the union representing all the states, but with the south and the southern way of life.

Dixie
I wish I was in Dixie, Hoo-ray! Hoo-ray!
In Dixie land I'll take my stand
To live and die in Dixie.
Away, away, away down south in Dixie!
Away, away, away down south in Dixie!

(*This is not the full text of the song.*)

Directions: Answer the questions about southerners and "Dixie".

1. Why did southerners who disapproved of slavery keep their opinions to themselves?

_____

2. Why did southerners want more slaves?

_____

3. What are the words on some southern Civil War monuments?

_____

4. What "stand" is referred to in *Dixie*?

☐ stand for slavery   ☐ stand against slavery   ☐ stand for cotton

5. "Secede" means to

☐ quit   ☐ fight   ☐ withdraw

Reading Comprehension

Name: _____

Fact Or Opinion?

Directions: Read the numbered sentences and put an x in the corresponding numbered boxes to tell whether each sentence gives a fact or an opinion.

1. *Dixie* is a beautiful song!

2. It was written in 1859 by a man named Daniel Emmett, who died in 1904.

3. The song became a ralllying cry for southerners because it showed where their loyalties were.

4. I think their loyalty to slavery was absolutely wrong!

5. These four states where people owned slaves did not secede from the Union: Delaware, Maryland, Kentucky and Missouri.

6. The people in these states certainly made the right moral choice.

7. The ownership of one human being by another is absolutely and totally wrong under any circumstances.

8. In the states that did not secede from the union, some people fought for the Union and others fought for the Confederacy of Southern States.

9. Sometimes brothers fought against brothers on opposite sides of the war.

10. What a horrible situation to be in!

1. ☐ Fact ☐ Opinion

2. ☐ Fact ☐ Opinion

3. ☐ Fact ☐ Opinion

4. ☐ Fact ☐ Opinion

5. ☐ Fact ☐ Opinion

6. ☐ Fact ☐ Opinion

7. ☐ Fact ☐ Opinion

8. ☐ Fact ☐ Opinion

9. ☐ Fact ☐ Opinion

10. ☐ Fact ☐ Opinion

Reading Comprehension

Name: _____

Review

Although they were outnumbered, most southerners were convinced they could win the Civil War. The white population of the southern states was 5.5 million. The population was 18.9 million in the 19 states that stayed with the Union. Despite these odds, southerners felt history was on their side.

After all, the Colonists had been the underdogs against the British and had won the war for independence. Europeans also felt that Lincoln could not force the South to re-join the Union. The United Netherlands had successfully seceded from Spain. Greece had seceded from Turkey. Europeans were laying odds that two countries would take the place of what had once been the United States.

Directions: Answer the questions and work the puzzle.

1. What was the difference in population between the Union and Confederate states?

   _____

2. The main idea is:

   Although they were outnumbered, many people here and abroad felt the South would win the Civil War.

   Because they were outnumbered, the South knew winning the Civil War was a very long shot.

Across
4. They won the War of Independence against England.
5. Did Europeans believe the South would win the war?
6. _____teen states belonged to the Union.

Down
1. Slaveowners lived in this area of the country.
2. The president during the Civil War.
3. To withdraw from the Union.

Copyright © 1994 American Education Publishing Co.

Recognizing Details: Fun With Photography

The word photography means "writing with light." "Photo" is from the Greek word **photos** which means light. "Graphy" is from the Greek word **graphic** which means writing. Cameras don't literally write pictures of course. Instead, they imprint an image onto a piece of film.

Even the most sophisticated camera is basically a box with a piece of light-sensitive film inside a box. The box has a hole at the opposite end from the film. The light enters the box from the hole—the camera's lens—and shines on the surface of the film to create a picture. The picture that's created on the film is the image the camera's lens is pointed toward.

A **lens** is a circle of glass that is thinner at the edges and thicker in the center. The outer edges of the lens collect the light rays and draw them together at the center of the lens.

The **shutter** helps control the amount of light that enters the lens. Too much light will make the picture too light. Too little light will result in a dark picture. Electronic flash—either built into the camera or attached to the top of it—provides light when needed.

Cameras with automatic electronic flashes will provide the additional light automatically. Electronic flashes—or "flashes" as they are often called—require batteries. If your automatic flash or flash attachment quits working, a dead battery is probably the cause.

Directions: Answer the questions about photography.

1. From what language is the word "photography" derived?

___

2. Where is the camera lens thickest?

___

3. What do the outer edges of the lens do?

___

4. When is a flash needed?

___

5. What does the shutter do?

___

Comprehension: Photography Terms

Like other good professionals, photographers make their craft look easy. Their skill—like that of the graceful ice skater—comes from years of practice. Where skaters develop a sense of balance, photographers develop an "eye" for pictures. They can make important technical decisions about photographing, or "shooting," a particular scene in the twinkling of an eye.

It's interesting to know some of the technical language that professional photographers use. "Angle of view" refers to the angle from which a photograph is taken. "Depth of field" is the distance between the nearest point and the farthest point in a photo that is in focus.

"Filling the frame" refers to the amount of space the object being photographed takes up in the picture. A close-up picture of a dog, flower or person would fill the frame. A far-away picture would not.

"ASA" refers to the speed of different types of films. "Speed" means the film's sensitivity to light. The letters ASA stand for the American Standards Association. Film manufacturers give their films ratings of 200ASA, 400ASA, etc. to indicate film speed. The higher the number on the film, the higher its sensitivity to light and the faster its speed. The faster its speed, the better it will be at clearly capturing sports images and other action shots.

Directions: Answer the questions about photography terms.

1. Name another term for photographing. _____

2. This is the distance between the nearest point and the farthest point of a photo that's in focus. _____

3. This refers to the speed of different types of film. _____

4. A close-up picture of someone's face would

   ☐ provide depth of field   ☐ create an ASA   ☐ fill the frame

5. To photograph a swimming child, which film speed is better?

   ☐ 200ASA   ☐ 400ASA

Reading Comprehension

Name: _____

Following Directions: Photography Puzzler

Directions: Use the facts you have learned about photography to work the puzzle.

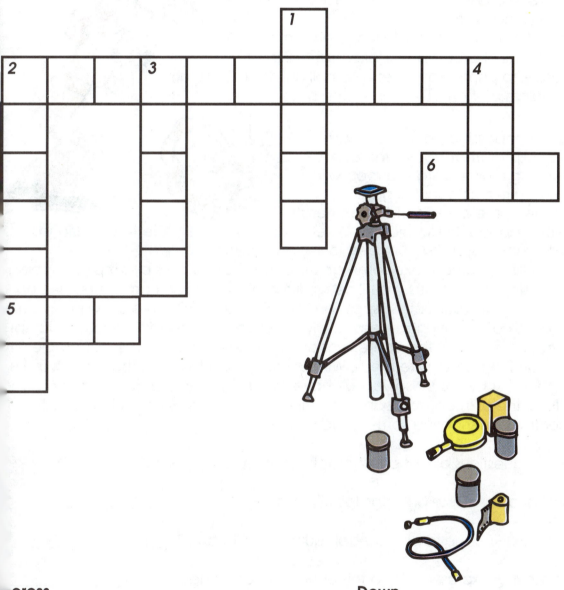

cross
A film's speed indicates its _____ to light.
Good photographers develop an ___ for pictures.
Stands for the American Standards Association.

Down
1. This is what the Greek word "photos" means.
2. This helps control the amount of light entering the lens.
3. This term refers to the film's sensitivity to light.
4. Would a close-up picture of a cat fill the frame?

27

Copyright © 1994 American Education Publishing Co.

Comprehension: Photographing Animals

Animals are a favorite subject of many young photographers. Cats, dogs, hamsters and other pets top the list, followed by zoo animals and the occasional lizard.

Because it's hard to get them to sit still and "perform on command," many professional photographers joke that—given a choice—they will refuse to photograph pets or small children. There **are** ways around the problem of short attention spans, however.

One way to get an appealing portrait of a cat or dog is to hold a biscuit or treat above the camera. The animal's longing look toward the food will be captured by the camera as a soulful gaze. Because it's above the camera— out of the camera's range—the treat won't appear in the picture. When you show the picture to your friends afterwards, they will be impressed by your pets loving expression.

If you are using fast film, you can take some good, quick shots of pets by simply snapping a picture right after calling their names. You'll get a different expression from your pet using this technique. Depending on your pet's disposition, the picture will capture an inquisitive expression or possibly a look of annoyance—especially if you've awakened Rover from a nap!

To photograph zoo animals, put the camera as close to the animal's cage as possible so you can shoot between the bars or wire mesh. Wild animals don't respond the same way as pets—after all, they don't know you!—so you will have to be more patient to capture a good shot. If it's legal to feed the animals, you can get their attention by having a friend toss them treats as you concentrate on shooting some good pictures.

Directions: Answer the questions about photographing animals.

1. Why do some professionals dislike photographing animals? _____

2. What speed film should you use to photograph quick-moving pets? _____

3. To capture a pet's loving expression, hold this out of camera range. _____

4. For a good picture of zoo animals

   ☐ get close to the cage   ☐ stand back from the cage

5. To get a zoo animal's attention, who should toss them treats?

   ☐ the photographer   ☐ a friend   ☐ a zoo keeper

Reading Comprehension

Name: _____

Generalization

A generalization is a statement of principle that applies in many different situations.

Directions: Read each passage and circle the valid generalization.

1. Most people can quickly be taught to use a simple camera. However, it takes time, talent and a good eye to learn to take professional quality photographs. Patience is another quality that good photographers must possess. Those who photograph nature often will wait hours to get just the right light or shadow in their pictures.

    a. Anyone can learn to use a camera.
    b. Any patient person can become a good photographer.
    c. Good photographers have a good eye for pictures.

2. Photographers such as Diane Arbus, who photograph strange or odd people, also must wait for just the right picture. Many "people photographers" stake out a busy city sidewalk and study the faces of crowds. Then they must leap up quickly and ask to take a picture—or sneakily take one without being observed. Either way, it's not an easy task!

    a. Staking out a busy city sidewalk is a boring task.
    b. "People photographers" must be patient people and good observers.
    c. Sneak photography is not a nice thing to do to strangers.

3. Whether the subject is nature or humans, many photographers insist that dawn is the best time to take pictures. The light is clear at this early hour, and mist may still be in the air. The mist gives these early morning photos a haunting, "other world" quality that is very appealing.

    a. Morning mist gives an unusual quality to most outdoor photographs.
    b. Photographers all agree that dawn is the best time to take pictures.
    c. Misty light is always important in taking all pictures.

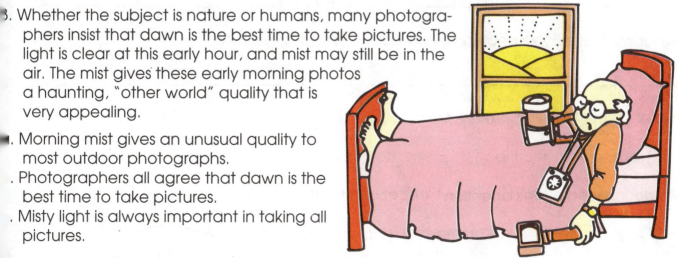

Comprehension: Camera Care

Camera dealers say many amateur photographers should take better care of their cameras. Too often, people carelessly leave expensive cameras lying out where young children or pets can get hold of them. They fail to put cameras back into the carrying cases that protect them. They take them to the beach and leave them lying in the sand. Another way people ruin their cameras is by leaving them for days inside a hot car.

Because they must carry so many attachments, professional photographers keep their cameras inside a large, soft shoulder bag. The bag provides extra protection for the camera, which is also protected by its camera case.

Inside the bag are compartments for film, extra lenses and other attachments. Other equipment inside a professional photographer's bag may include the following: lens hood, cable release, filters and holder, cleaning cloth and screw driver. A photographer's bag is filled with all sorts of interesting things! Flashlights, pens, tape and sometimes a sandwich for lunch may fill out the odd assortment of objects. In addition, many photographers carry a tripod to set the camera on for still pictures. Can you see why photographers usually develop strong arm and shoulder muscles?

Directions: Answer the questions about caring for and storing cameras.

1. Name four ways people abuse their cameras.

1.) _____ 2.) _____

3.) _____ 4.) _____

2. What do professional photographers carry their equipment in?

_____

3. Which of the following is **not** in a photographer's bag?

☐ lens hood   ☐ tripod   ☐ lens filters

4. Photographers often develop which set of muscles?

☐ legs and feet   ☐ arms and shoulders   ☐ head and neck

Reading Comprehension Name: _____

Generalization

Directions: Read each passage and circle the valid generalization.

1. Professional photographers know it's important to keep their cameras clean and in good working order. Amateur photographers should make sure theirs are, too. However, to take good care of your camera, you must first understand the equipment. Camera shop owners say at least half the "defective" cameras people bring in simply need to have the battery changed!

a. Cameras are delicate and require constant care so they will work properly.
b. Many problems amateurs have are caused by lack of familiarity with their equipment.
c. Amateur photographers don't know how their cameras work.

2. Once a year, some people take their cameras to a shop to be cleaned. Most never have them cleaned at all! Those who know how can clean their cameras themselves. To avoid scratching the lens, they should use the special cloths and tissues professionals rely on. Amateurs are warned never to unloosen screws, bolts or nuts inside the camera.

a. The majority of amateur photographers never bother to have their cameras cleaned.
b. Cleaning a camera can be tricky and should be left to professionals.
c. It's hard to find the special cleaning cloths professionals use.

3. Another simple tip from professionals—make sure your camera works **before** you take it on vacation. They suggest taking an entire roll of film and having it developed before your trip. That way, if necessary, you'll have time to have the lens cleaned or other repairs made.

a. Check out your camera beforehand to make sure it's in good working order before you travel.
b. Vacation pictures are often disappointing because the camera needs repairing.
c. Take at least one roll of film along on every vacation.

31

Reading Comprehension

Name: _____

Review

Using A Darkroom

The room where photographs are developed is called a "darkroom." Can you guess why? The room must be completely dark so that light does not get on the film as it is being developed. Because of the darkness and the chemicals used in the developing process, it's important to follow certain darkroom safety procedures.

To avoid shocks while in the darkroom, never touch light switches with wet hands. To avoid touching chemicals, use tongs to transfer prints from one chemical solution to another. When finished with the chemicals, put them back in their bottles. Never leave chemicals out in trays once the developing process is completed.

To avoid skin irritation from chemicals, wipe down all counter tops and surfaces when finished. Another sensible precaution—make sure you have everything you need **before** exposing the film to begin the developing process. Any light that enters the darkroom as you leave to get a forgotten item can ruin the pictures being developed.

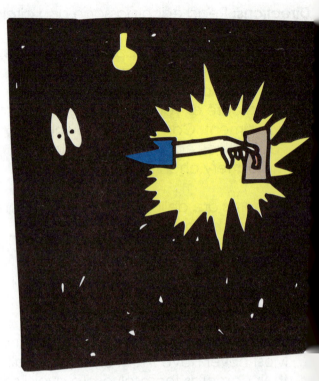

Directions: Answer the questions about using a darkroom.

1. Which generalization is correct?
a. Developing pictures is a time-consuming and difficult process.
b. It's dangerous to develop pictures in a darkroom.
c. Sensible safety procedures are important for darkroom work.

2. Give directions for working with photography chemicals.

3. Give the most important detail on how to make sure pictures aren't ruined in the darkroom.